BEST DAD JOKE BOOK EVER

Cringy, Yet Oh So Satisfying

Damon Wiseley

Every father should remember one day his son will follow his example, not his advice.

CHARLES KETTERING

If I ever lost my mood ring I'm not sure how I'd feel about that.

◆ ◆ ◆

Did you hear about the movie constipation? It never came out.

◆ ◆ ◆

Documentaries about beavers are the best damn programming ever.

◆ ◆ ◆

When does a joke become a Dad joke? When it's apparent.

◆ ◆ ◆

I told my waiter the coffee tastes like dirt. He said it was fresh ground.

◆ ◆ ◆

What's another name for someone else's cheese? Nacho cheese

◆ ◆ ◆

Why did the blind man fall down the well? Because he couldn't see that well.

◆ ◆ ◆

What's a spicy name for an old girlfriend? Old Bae

◆ ◆ ◆

What's the best time to go to the Dentist? Tooth-thirty

◆ ◆ ◆

Braille is pretty easy to learn once you get a feel for it.

◆ ◆ ◆

How many tickles does it take to make an octopus laugh? Ten-ticles

◆ ◆ ◆

My friend was murdered after making fun of a man named Terry. The coroner said he died from "**dissin**-Terry".

◆ ◆ ◆

What do you call a person with no body and no nose? Nobody nose

◆ ◆ ◆

Why don't crabs give to charity? Because they're shellfish.

◆ ◆ ◆

Did you hear about the cross-eyed teacher? He couldn't control his pupils.

◆ ◆ ◆

What's another name for a pile
of cats? A meow-tain

◆ ◆ ◆

What did one nut say to the other nut
he was chasing? I'ma cashew!

◆ ◆ ◆

What do you call a man with no
shins? Toe knee (Tony)

◆ ◆ ◆

Did you know that nearly everyone
hates blankets? Of course, that's
just a blanket statement.

◆ ◆ ◆

Why did the coffee file a police report?
Because he got mugged.

◆ ◆ ◆

Did you hear the rumor about butter?
Never mind, I don't want to spread it.

◆ ◆ ◆

I ate a clock the other day. It was very time consuming but I went back for seconds.

◆ ◆ ◆

What did the pirate say on his 80th birthday? Aye-m-atey

◆ ◆ ◆

Why did the turkey cross the road?
Never mind it's a foul joke.

◆ ◆ ◆

Why is Apples headquarters so dark?
Because they refuse to install Windows.

◆ ◆ ◆

How do ducks pay for things? They just put it on their bill

◆ ◆ ◆

Why did the golfer wear two pairs of pants? In case he got a hole in one.

◆ ◆ ◆

What did the baby corn ask moma corn? Where's popcorn?

◆ ◆ ◆

Why shouldn't you wear your watch around your waste? It's a waste of time.

◆ ◆ ◆

What do you call a small mom?
A minimum

◆ ◆ ◆

Why are pediatricians so easily upset?
They have little patience.

◆ ◆ ◆

What was the first English tax
collectors name? Sir charge

◆ ◆ ◆

What did the stir-fry say to the crab?
Don't wok away from me

◆ ◆ ◆

Why won't Steve Harvey talk to his
wife? They're having a family fued.

◆ ◆ ◆

Why does the baker get mad when
you take away his toast? He's
lack toast intolerant.

◆ ◆ ◆

I have an extreme fear of escalators,
so I'm taking steps to get better.

◆ ◆ ◆

What do you call someone who doesn't
celebrate Christmas? Eggnog-stic

◆ ◆ ◆

How do you catch a squirrel?
Show him your nuts.

◆ ◆ ◆

Divorce is tough! My friend left his
wife Ruth and now he's Ruthless.

◆ ◆ ◆

What do Hawaiians say when they
burn their food? I should've used
aloha temperature.

◆ ◆ ◆

Ben Franklin was trying to figure out how lighting works. Then it struck him.

◆ ◆ ◆

Why did the entomologist throw butter out the window? To see a butter-fly.

◆ ◆ ◆

Did you hear about the cow killed by a tornado? It was an udder disaster.

◆ ◆ ◆

Why was the broom always late to work? It kept over-sweeping.

◆ ◆ ◆

How could you cut the ocean in half? With a sea-saw.

◆ ◆ ◆

How do you explain you're going on a solo road trip with a bear? Just bear with me.

◆ ◆ ◆

What do you call someone who will do anything for spaghetti? A pasta-tute

◆ ◆ ◆

What's a coal minors favorite type of art? Minecraft

◆ ◆ ◆

What does the pepper say before going on vacation? See you next season

◆ ◆ ◆

What does the cow say when the bull insults her? How dair-y

◆ ◆ ◆

Why doesn't anyone eat clowns?
They taste funny.

◆ ◆ ◆

Why is the library the tallest building in every city? It's got the most stories.

◆ ◆ ◆

How do you make a hotdog stand?
Take away his chair.

◆ ◆ ◆

What did the duck say to the comedian? You quack me up.

◆ ◆ ◆

What's black, white, and read all over? The newspaper

◆ ◆ ◆

Have you ever played silent tennis? It's just like tennis but without the racquet.

◆ ◆ ◆

Dad, are you going to take a bath? No, I'm gonna leave it where it is.

◆ ◆ ◆

What's another name for a 12-inch nose? A foot

◆ ◆ ◆

Is it okay if I watch TV dad? Sure, just don't turn it on.

◆ ◆ ◆

Me: What's up Dad? Dad: The opposite of down

◆ ◆ ◆

How do I look Dad? With your eyes.

◆ ◆ ◆

Can I go to the bathroom? I don't
know, can you?

◆ ◆ ◆

Should I get a haircut? No, you
should get them all cut.

◆ ◆ ◆

What's another name for fake
spaghetti? Impasta

◆ ◆ ◆

Dad, my foot is killing me. Don't worry;
it'll feel better when it stops hurting.

◆ ◆ ◆

Paper jokes are **tear**able

Call me later Dad. Okay later

◆ ◆ ◆

Dad, can you make me lunch?
Bam! You're lunch.

◆ ◆ ◆

Dad, how do you feel? With my hands

◆ ◆ ◆

What's the fastest drink? Milk, it's pasteurized before you can see it.

◆ ◆ ◆

Dad: I'm going to take a bath in milk. Me: Pasteurized? Dad: No, only up to my neck.

◆ ◆ ◆

Can a nose dance? Only if it has a boogie in it.

◆ ◆ ◆

Why kind of fruit has big weddings? Cant-**elope**

◆ ◆ ◆

How do you find out when a planet
dies? Look in the orbit-uary

◆ ◆ ◆

Why do batteries feel lonely? Because
they're never included

◆ ◆ ◆

Can you put my shoes on? No,
my feet are too big.

◆ ◆ ◆

Why is the banker so depressed?
He just lost interest.

◆ ◆ ◆

How can you always be on time?
Sit on your watch.

◆ ◆ ◆

Can a frog jump higher than a house?
Yeah sure, houses can't jump.

◆ ◆ ◆

Why are restaurants on the moon
bad? There's no atmosphere.

◆ ◆ ◆

Why does no one laugh at pizza jokes?
Because they're too cheesy.

◆ ◆ ◆

Are you a grape that got stepped on?
Because you let out a little wine.

◆ ◆ ◆

Should I go on the almond diet?
Or is that just nuts?

◆ ◆ ◆

Dad: Never trust trees son. Son: Why not? Dad: Because they're shady.

◆ ◆ ◆

Would you like to hear a construction joke….that's okay, I'm still working on it.

◆ ◆ ◆

Where do dogs shop for new tails? Retail stores

◆ ◆ ◆

What's brown and sticky? A stick

◆ ◆ ◆

What do you call a tree that looks like a chicken? Poul-tree

◆ ◆ ◆

How did the scarecrow win an award?
For being out standing in his field.

◆ ◆ ◆

What do you call an alligator wearing
a vest? An investigator.

◆ ◆ ◆

I tried to use a broken pencil
but it was pointless.

◆ ◆ ◆

Why are airport jokes boring?
They're too plane.

◆ ◆ ◆

Did you hear about the kidnapping?
It's okay, he woke up.

◆ ◆ ◆

Who does a pharaoh talk to when
he's sad? His mummy

◆ ◆ ◆

What's another name for an
Alaskan dog? Chilidog

◆ ◆ ◆

That circus fire was huge. Yeah,
it was "in-tents."

◆ ◆ ◆

I dreamt I was a muffler last night.
I woke up exhausted.

◆ ◆ ◆

I found out the girl who stole my diary had
died. My thoughts are with her family.

◆ ◆ ◆

My family left me because they thought I was too obsessed with racing horses. ...And they're off!

❖ ❖ ❖

My waiter asked me if I want a box for my leftover food. I told him it's not worth fighting over.

❖ ❖ ❖

I didn't always like having a beard, but then it grew on me.

Never trust an atom. They make up everything.

❖ ❖ ❖

A book hit my head. I've only my shelf to blame.

❖ ❖ ❖

A man fell into an upholstery
machine. He's fully recovered.

◆ ◆ ◆

Cows have hooves because they lactose.

◆ ◆ ◆

I used to suffer from soap addiction,
but I'm clean now.

Running with bagpipes will get you kilt.

◆ ◆ ◆

Alert! Police toilet stolen. Cops
have nothing to go on.

◆ ◆ ◆

Ban pre-shredded cheese. Make America Grate again.

◆ ◆ ◆

If you have any bowling puns, spare me.

◆ ◆ ◆

A cow stumbled into a marijuana field. The stakes have never been higher.

◆ ◆ ◆

The past present and future walked into a bar. It was tense!

◆ ◆ ◆

Resistance training is when you refuse to go to the gym.

◆ ◆ ◆

Puns about poop aren't my favorite, but they're a solid number 2.

◆ ◆ ◆

I buy my guns from a guy named T-rex. He's a small arms dealer.

◆ ◆ ◆

Puns about communism aren't funny unless everyone gets them.

◆ ◆ ◆

Of course communism was never going to work. There were red flags everywhere.

◆ ◆ ◆

A bike in town keeps running me over. It's a vicious cycle.

◆ ◆ ◆

Bad puns? That's how eye roll.

◆ ◆ ◆

Reintarnation is when hillbillies come back to life.

◆ ◆ ◆

My relationship with whiskey
is on the rocks.

◆ ◆ ◆

Beer is a gateway drug to aspirin.

◆ ◆ ◆

If you suck at playing the trumpet
that's probably why.

◆ ◆ ◆

Why couldn't the alcoholic become a
lawyer? He couldn't pass the bar.

◆ ◆ ◆

Research shows that 6 out of 7
dwarves aren't happy.

◆ ◆ ◆

I can tell if people are judgemental
just by looking at them.

◆ ◆ ◆

I ordered a chicken and an egg on the internet to see which one comes first.

◆ ◆ ◆

After my girlfriend became a vegan I felt like I'd never seen herbivore.

◆ ◆ ◆

I'm friends with 25 letters of the alphabet, but I don't know Y.

◆ ◆ ◆

If a parsley farmer loses a lawsuit can his wages be garnished?

◆ ◆ ◆

If cats could text you back
THEY WOULDN'T.

◆ ◆ ◆

Kleptomaniacs always take things literally.

◆ ◆ ◆

The man who invented velcro has did...RIP.